THE RADIO ARCHITECT

TWIN QUANTUM PARADOX

KARANVIR SINGH

ISBN 979-888530299-9

My father was an Architect .... a little mannerful man and a mighty ironic head....

When i would as God my castle i will tell i wanna meet him a one more time.

Ladies & Gentlemen !

"*JS Rahi. (PWRMDC, Punjab)*"

(Mommy will turn off the RADIO)

A Literal Thanks To my Great Seniors My Two Grand Fathers, S. Lashkar Singh & Late. S. Harbans Singh

My best support in times of distress Ms Manvir, Ms Rajvir & S. Gurminder Singh

Thank You & See Ya'll For Remmittances...

A huge Market Applause and Credit to Radio Services from Bloomberg Radio NY, Voice OF America WA, BBC World Service London,KKOL Seattle, KDOW Palo Alto, RMF Hip Hop, Cracow Poland, Wallstreet & CITIBANK Inc., CIA, Government Of India, United States Senate, United Nations, G7, G20, IMF, ECB, NSE ($) HT Media, Radio Today, RBNL & Starbucks, Cafe Coffee Day, Novotel Juhu, Prithvi Theatre, all my ventures.

My Constant support , MY Education, MY Institutions, My Crop...

+ University Of Adelaid, SAE (School Of Audio Engineering) USA, UK, EU,Canada , UAE & Australia

+University Of Toronto, Edx, Alison.com for my Journalism Studies.

+AAT Mumbai, Chennai

"***Ms Shobhana Bhartiya, Chairperson , HT Media Ltd...****A BIG Shout OUT To the most dire and practical of industrious Woman Leaders , she knows magic with words & pictures. At the epicentre business at HT she is the BASEBAND of Every Innovation.*

HT- My Cadillac Story , My Mother-God. "

Kishore Banan, who shaped us at the Audio School with hs supreme intellect and technical faculties. No doubt he is a home grown Genius and he shall keep us busy till we depart from the Terminal. Kudos!

My School , Toddlers' Home Study Hall (THSH, Hoshiarpur, Punjab.)

[Govt. Senior Secondary School, Hoshiarpur , SSC] & Punjab School Education Board.

Note For Baby Guntas & Baby Gunreet:

"***"The day this reaches you i will be again on the rollercoaster with God!" - KV***"

Note For Baby Agampreet:

"WE LOVE YOU , you are our gift to eternity....and God is Real." - KV

Eternal Thanks to My Esteemed Guests On the book and thier phenomenol HABITS.

Thank You: Team FINBLUE IN-US (R5I900)

Thank You : PaperBlue Isc. (Our eBlue Partners)

Thank You Wikipedia, Keep Supporting Free Culture. (Donate)

To Kalyani N. , My Umbrella & Eternal Cardinal Since 1987. Ooops....(She's is a Strawberry) THE FBI SAYS She is IN FURIOUS! She joins us from Mumbai, India on the book....Enjoy The True Pageant!!

Jazzy B, The Only Artist I would ever listen to on my Youtube....Ummm....He ROCKS!- Siddharth Rastogi(Comments Post 3 Black Label Pegs, two Chicken Afghani & a Benson Cigrette....if i remember)

Sid ! Love :) Get The Cheque! ($)

Dr. Amit Barde (From the SAE, Mumbai Batch Mates) A Research Fellow & Sound Designer in Auckland. A cult figure in his own sphere of knowledge and a powerfull resource at trade. May The Light Be with You!

KJ Singh, A Prime Industry Man and the Backstage guy who has inspired us since INCEPTION.

Is that ok KV......????.......(From The HOUSE **Dr. Sonia Parasnis**) [With Love] [**For The Multilateral Talks...I will one day call you from Heaven with G sitting NEXT to ME ...ummm..oh Sorry With GOD sitting next to ME......00:00 AM!**] BAE !! LoL :)

"Dr. Saab & S. Sarabjit Singh for being the GOD SENT!"

Waheguru Ji Ka Khalsa, Waheguru Ji Ki Fateh !

"11:46 PM

10-12-2021

[$] || Ik Onka'R , SatGu'r Prasa'd || [$]

Contents

Foreword

Yashvir Chauhan met me on the phone from Mumbai after a long time and connected together on a few Radio Sales Topics , I asked him to remind me of our days at Fever 104 FM Mumbai....He is a midland guy with great logical exuberance inside his minfd about business ad life.....I spoke to him a many time later and we discovered work and matter....

> ***"Today For Me "THE RADIO ARCHITECT" is a symbolic aftermath of many such conversations... - PaperBlue Bot (III3)"***

Mumbai has been the pirate club i saw many years and lived the instant coffee life and repealed the backstage bullion bubble. I see Radio as my Constant Partner Of Priviledge and here i thank the fish-luck on my tablle to turn up the Radio to my Firewall Once and For All !

Dial K for Kittens !

& @/// M for Musk !

Flight_by 4am- 21:00 Hrs (kv@media)

THE reflective articulation of a value system endorsed by the pragmatic technology , **CREATIVE EXPERIENCES** & Positive Mental Health, Radio is the king of good common times and the most sophisticated of media than ever before. I simply couldn't contrast in a world with or without Radio. This book will cancel most of the free time activities in a **Radio Station** and the space of selling ads and its social context.

I am desperate to unleash new behavioral patterns and the scale of algebraic operations a **Radio CEO**, **Radio Programmer or a Production Engineer** needs to stupify supporting musical evidence.

The Chaotic world of Indian FM Radio is a prose and commitment by all ways to excellence. I am pleased to furnish a natural cure to creating Radio Credit and its much wavering future has new skills , talents and functions to build it better.

"*Lets prove the vignette and move to illumination.*"

Radio is pre-eminent!

Preface

Ms. Rama Bijapurkar , The Bestselling Author of **We Are Like That Only**, has another book called **CUSTOMER IN THE BOARDROOM. When my first revelation came to me i was reading this book for Customer Based Business Strategy....She writes variably on two toned matters and a 6 Dimensional Business Space...**

> ***"I was a Hip Hop Listener.***
> ***I was 25 when my father passed away.***
> ***I was looking for 200 Dimes in a Common Business.***
> ***It was NOT a Nightmare."***

I took this book for real and took to trial some popular frameworks... The RADIO ARCHITECT is one question in Strategy, Market Leadership & A 100 Billion $ Party. Its Uncertainty, Segmentation & Preclosed Accounts that came looming in my head and I took the Economic Agenda of Propagating Acceleration and Navigation on the MAP.

The cursive undertaken from Broadcasting Equipments to Reach the Node That Is Playing My HIT SONG was a LION KING Battle. Very incredibly Rama Bijapurkar has made an imprint to let this book happen and mark me absent on my first day at work.

> ***""I am but my only pursuit. " - KV"***

Acknowledgements

"*This IS Drum 'n'Bass.......Cap That Radio FREQUENCY.....Play THE BASS TO THE TREBLE....-KV SINGH (Karanvir Singh)*"

Security Checklist: QQ10000-2000-E421900T

"*AXIA, Telos Aliance, Yamaha , KRK, JBL, Realme, Nuendo, Sony Vegas, O2R, AKG, Powergold, Google, Wikipedia, Wordpress, Meta, Instagram, Linked In, Youtube, Amazon, Flipkart.*

MY Startups IN STAR AGES..... ;) Since 2013......by the Silver Beach....- KV

BlueFedFin Ixc, Kapple Kape SXCi, Carrot Bay SXCi, Global Babies iVDx, eFox Computing GXi, Symbol One Fed iBXN, PaperBlue Isx, Gio Pix Network Canada EeXi.

***Virtual UNIVERSITY** : Kape Sine Teachings, Punjab (Blue School Initiative.)*

Project GoldFish SIX (6), Project NILE X1, Project SPECTRON'1S, Cloud CINDRELLAS, Cloud Blue Live &CEO Packets 3.0

World House 11XSS, Political Office [PoWT, PiWT, PIoWTR News Blog. - KV Singh (Karanvir Singh)

Our Banking Partners:

Yes Bank"

Prologue

+The Wierdos Singing my Raps in Poland,(KV) if you are smoking the LEGAL w@@d please feel free to turn up the 1K at the Dockkkkks....

Knock ...Knob...."?"

-Lions at BEACH .....Check out....its Khakis...!

+Fellas Reply: You have ordered your PIZZA from FRANCE.......!!! Novos!!! Adious !!!

_ARE WE CHARGED???

<><><><> ***CEO/CXO/CFO/CDO/CPO/CIO/CSO, CLO, CBO, HR, SM/PD/SE/ That CREATIVE Guy IN London ($).** <><><><>

"COVID 19CARD....
Lets Be Able To Maintain Distance.......!! -KV"

"-Queen's Road, Amritsar... THe CiTYYY Of My BirTH....!!!- CLO"

ONE

The Factory Settings

What is FM Radio ...? Hey....uooo in the pink....??? - @ibluekvsingh*

Frequency Modulation. There is Cut , Copy and Paste. But there's also **Z-Copy and Z-Space.** On that note I start your day at the academy, save yourself the rest of the automated events. Seat belts compulsory.

Here at the **"Executive Lounge"** there are prolific new ideas to super charge the audience from the requisition of the dawn and dusk of Radio.

There was a common thought that people love and relate to music as a therapist would give you a flying medical prescription so does the cycle hits the chart buster shows.

What an overview when it comes to sleeping on the Radio to merge the reflective cells into order. I am going to run you a **Radio Company....** but that is the desire to design a **Sequenced Music Radio Station** and a **Talk Less Music Format Station.** This is thru those millions of formats waiting to be explored by the attitude, competitiveness and excel excellence.

Am on a neutral ground...you play the best song of the day and the audience is bursting for humour symptoms. Now the talk comes then the light shines upon the word power the electronic capacity of a **Radio Voice** to un-root the nexus of an atmospheric pressure.

OK...No Sound Pressure.

A fitness test on Content on Radio can tell you what media is created and destroyed....The airtime of a radio promo comes with the propensity of junctions so many that the IQ Sells you the buyback of the work done on audio production within the Radio Company.

+ Project Browser (Why Radio Is an Audio Factory?)

When you first put the product knowledge on the table where the mixing engineer sits its empathetic to not understand the value system behind an Intelligent Media and the waste of time when fresh ideas loose sight from the anticipation in running the charts through the Channel.

Well a child bus would tell you the direction of the stream but hey the technology today has made Radio an Audio Factory.

> "***"Radio is but tons of Data yet a soothing Experiential Enigma."***"

Analytic Computation and that algorithm that works on scheduling the right rift of musical enigma.

+Music 1.0

The labels send music to the Radio Station. Every new release and each bite of parametric sound production to charge up audience on the promise of entertainment and information.

+ Promo Production

The ecstasy in the hands of a **Sound Engineer** /Sound Designer, Promo Producer is explicit. The freedom to turn imagination into a surround stage is the doctors remedy to produce ecstatic new sound stages and buffers. A Buffer **BOX** is the sound memory for the Audience. A promo will retain fresh notes and a sceptic engineering sedation. The Engineer takes it away.

+Music Scheduling

Why would you play what is popular in the 90s or go back still into Retro and play the **Proxy Tunes** from 50s, 60s or 70s....? Its an automatic channel selector in the minds of the audience you gotta tune the open settings for the playlist of the Day and Months to run. The management theory be that of pulling a bucket of creative pitching in one go. The **Alternate Channel Window (ACW)** is a gate between ruining competition and plucking from the wet garden. If a country has good music the passion for creation of a pro active pop-up can give you loads of enlightenment and institutional application of what **Reversible Radio Habits** mean.

+ The Psychotic Strategy

The complexity of Radio Tuners and the parallel audience is so effectively mission critical that you will bend the executive format to believe in the experiment. It could be declared more emphatically that the system generates great insightful data inside the core operations. Its the CEO leading from EQ to Effective Sales in 6 to 9 Figures a Week. That's Big Money CAD. A nuclear parsed by the sieve from a vacuum tube to reaching your smartphone Radio is Spear Headed to the arbitrary orders of a symphony in an auditorium.

The pragmatic search on data operations must be the sidereal activity of a Producer, RJ or a Programming Director. The Data thus holds intrinsic scientific propagation from being sorted and streamlined with the best sound picturesque. I think its 6 dB up. Ok....a strong signal is must.

+ The Virtual Programming Technique

As CEO you will need to question the **Radio Company** to organize its ability to innovate on the settling grounds with a brisk undertaking and ethnic disparity. The Virtual Methods can be rehearsed in our brains and the mapping would allow the listener to uncover strategic entertainment. That is the switch . The tuners know the frequency, the programmer must know the effective rate of listening. The collective creative intelligence can be sorted and reduced by thinking into a pie chart by true nominal values.

"My new theory is the **C-Suite CCF** (Centre Co-ordination Factorization) Application. A Radio CEO wont ask the bit to surprise his listener but rather challenge the broad category of what market is sounding like. The sound that shapes markets can be created inside the core radio production facilities."

"The Don Corleone Portrayal. - GODFATHER- For VOICE.

Al Pacino in GODFATHER for Leadership Ethics...The BLUNT...The SUBTLE !---Tonal Impulse Copy."

TWO

REAL TIME AUDIO SYSTEMS - LIVE RADIO

Why we wrote a constitution for media and the behavioral activities on the info line for running a Radio Network is precisely by the lack of invention and the bit response to read radio practically on base and finish a Billion $ business-market paradigm.

+Transpose:

The **Pitch Rule** is to play the sound f station to the tune of its Transpose Field. That field is deep because that is what produces the decision tree for the **CEO** and Staff to work around and turn the knob on the rivals in business.

The value of audio events is a quantum problem. When the Promo /Song/ Jingle / Ad runs for the first time the lateral part is definite. The calculations in between the choice of the audience served by the cloud is intrinsic and on a Quantize Function (QF).

+ 5000K -ve Digit Permutation

The decimated result of creating content and running it to the clock is a cookie building technique that can reduce the Digital Damage to **Cloud** that plays the Programming. The flexibility containing the **Data** and the **Meta-Beta Media Content (MBMC)** is thus together on the table that which the CEO needs the most.

+ Combination OF Powers- News Control

There is a Circular Formula to judge your Creative Data, Music Playlists and the Frantic Production in the Studio. The Elements used on a Promo can tell you why the most practical of Creative Officers use the right and left brain symbology to adopt a Creative and play it on air.

+ Pre-Cast Channels

At the side-real programme when a data centre seeks rest is the audible experience the channel is Pre Cast at Prime Times and at the Odds when a permanent initial investment in content is higher than the selective music experience the job is half done.

On a regular scale a 6dB push to acknowledge a full volume cast out or a shout out from the front by the Jock is very impressive.

+ Repeat Cost

Dangers of broadcasting repeat content is not an issue that the whole proposition is backed by economics. Repeat the Theatre in a unfamiliar fashion or package to the industry standard faucet to tighten grip over competition by making familiarization of an audio stream over your Network. The Radio CEO would play all but the Daisy Hunter on the set. The studio output must negate an analytical approach to a great feat and the No. 1 Position offset.

+ Psy Definitions - Uplink - Downlink

Radio by far as a standard can be compared to an individual by aggregate of **Behavioral Exchange of Entertainment (BEE).**

> "***BEE** means that the mp3 definition of audio is not the gadget grab or the lossless format doesn't carry a liquid cell.*
>
> ***BEE** carries a node to node data insight carrier and that which will collate to the interactive state of the Radio between **Transmission and Catching a Listener.**"*

Radio is irritable, Radio can get Depression. All but laughable. A Radio CEO knows the operational business strength of his spectrum from a drive and find motivations alongside AI and BI to be a New Age Programmer. New Age BEE also holds effective Rate Capture Properties to Market the Radio Brand You Own in the best possible manner. The **ECHO** is real, the technology can give you the next big revolution. There is Internet Radio and FM can work on the lining to broaden analogue broadcasters to gain momentum and pass thru the bubble by a **100 Cents**. That gets a BIG Money CAD introduction in the chapters to come.

THREE

PsYCHOLOGY OF AUDIO FRAMEWORK- BY THE DATA CENTRE GUY!

The development and utilization of Radio has come out from personality desires to intellectual alertness and a motivational driver. That goes into making the 80% of the Day for Music on Music Stations and Going 40% music on Talk Station. 80 % and 40 % are worth 10 Billion $ and How the Music Plays its manner and **'PSY'** Inference on Listeners the Drive becomes stronger and stronger. That's called buying tickets to a Radio Concert.

Radio as an individual can get depression and analytical depression. The void formed by habitual music rather than Cognitive Music and the same order serves to the Jock who would sell it to the air command.

Early intuitive formats in **Music** can have three broad virtual categories ;

1. Rip and Run (Ask A Listener)
2. Test and Run (Mask A Listener)
3. Run and Execute. (Create A Listener)

The above division is cognitive and once you start thinking of progress on your station , a **Chief Marketing Officer** who can interpret the differential between the reaction and the fruition of the concept can lay his money and faith on this belt.

Radio can make you feel wanted. The love and affection that a listener gets from the mood value of the station , good social interactions and an established audience are the free market tools.

To protect the freedom of the medium in question its an attitude issue that I find has been screaming at the radio industry.

Some Radio CEOs have no-head adjustment ... Only the intelligent survives.

"The subscriber you have called is currently Busy."

+ Statistical Knowledge

One of the basic frames in audio is the impact of statistical knowledge of the Audio Cloud. Its getting advanced and the **Ethernet** not only copies the imprint but the entire game can be reversed using a statistical model to cure better engaging Music & Talk experience.

The efficacy level can be monitored on the **P&L** by a division of multiple factors like Audience Measurement, Market Value and Common Sense to add to the party for a **Programming Director** / Station Manager.

A No. 1 Radio Station/Network is largely consumed by the lateral creative power coming from the Scheduling Desk to the On-Air Capabilities of the Team in question.

More good news, Radio Networks can feed the stream with highly electric content which must pledge to Infotainment and Entertainment.

IT capabilities add to the filament for more light in the entertainment space. The recognized formula to success is commonly a nudge in the backdrop of a Great Radio Show. The best **SFX** the best Voice the final countdown to the brink of successful transition counts on the objective the Radio Network is Communicating to the Audience.

Radio stands out for its own **Statistical Power** and Insights from the **Revenues*** generated by the Sales Team.

What an investor is thinking or what the Advertiser has in demand is a must copy command to reload **Text Mining and Data Analysis.**

Audio Data is a newly embedded **Cloud Service** that can compliment the fraction of calculative progress for the slow movers. But a fast adaptation to the working of the Infra is even more essential than pace naturally subjected to the Market Assembly/Competition.

A break even scenario can be seen within the game in the right jurisdiction to enroll more extensive content.

Radio Stream is the picture behind the mother tincture that goes in the making of the Programming of the Station/Network.

A complete station gives ample choice of production value to the Advertiser and a base footprint is established via the native linguistic abilities of the Station to pamper the shared stream and the Fabric of the Talk Content Chosen.

A rear choice can be the axiomatic process to play the different Era's of Music, Celebrity Talk , Promo Production and Personality Crash on your competitor.

The **Solid State Geometry** of the **Radio Network** is easily exploitable from the upper view to all of the Daily Management and Creation Process.

What happens with this geometry is the turn table formatting of the equity and the reference point of the Market getting stronger. A Market for Radio is the Jump Suite to Contractions and Frequency Mapping to deliver high quality **Audio Experience** which itself is Intelligent, Entertaining and Unique. A No. 1 Radio show is all about the **Connective Psychology (CP)** that works well with Radio and the Theatrical Exuberance of the Medium which is up by 10 basis points from the Equation of Liquid Market.

+ Mobility & Deployment - Neo Architecture (NA)

A fine estimate of the generalization of the Radio Industry is hidden in between Mobility and Deployment. Mobility is incredible source of new progress and an equitable asset while learning the Algorithm that will process for you the sync in the Cloud.

Mobile phones with connectivity attract most of the Radio Listeners with a **FM** Receiver on their Mobile Phones ...that is extensive and exterior to the inner functioning of the Radio Materials.

While induction to new capabilities that would amplify the **Network Status** in the Server Room. The server room the **CTI** are comprehensive belts to accomplish a paradigm turnover for the Agency working inside the Radio Network. Its an essential boom for the type of advertiser who would get the meaningful labour getting rewarded by just an algorithm and the fine placement of your content on the parameters of the streaming media.

The **Broadcasting Network** that can acquire the comprehensive and the in-comprehensive data generated at the Station can also win the battle of configuring the best possible **Data Chains** and **Analytic Corridor** from the pleasant and willful assimilation of **Mobility and Deployment.** A Radio CEO and CPO can both be sorted inside their minds to accomplish revenue targets and Creative funnels can level up the game to challenge any competitor in the **Market.**

Music has a unique perception and not all people like the same kind of music. Here the mobility becomes a first rated option to induct more **Lead Solutions** , Industry Specific Call Rates and Sales & **Service Calls** are very well authored.

A lot of promise goes into the making of a stable and strong FM Signal and has to be a mercurial job to automate the **Single Thread Processing** to **Hybrid** and **Conventional Processing Dialogues.**

A Radio Company must have its survival kit and be free to chose the most insidious of the tasks to promote its stakeholders at all times. A stakeholder is the FIN bubble and the Induction Algorithm is the key to opening **New Age Digital Market Assembly (NADMA).**

FOUR

AUDIO RESERVES & PRAGMATIC PROGRAMMING-AN IOT 1.0 EDIT!

> "*"What actually looks likes an Apple in the studio for the Jockey can just be the tool to encroach over the Competitor."-KV* "

Primary and Secondary markets are tuples from a united application theory. What goes into the making of these two Markets is the **Territorial Rating System** (TRS).The two markets operate on Margins and Targets from its close affiliation to the societal norms and entertainment criteria. A Bollywood Station for example is more crucial to people in the range of expectations and proliferation of moods they want to listen to. That is the Pragmatic Call and its under the service parameters to opt the best of the challenge to entertain both the markets. Its the crucial role of the BOT that **Radio Programming** plays to the audience and sales services are affected by the game plane and the goals set by the Administration.

A working Pragmatic Model must include a **Hedge FUND Risk** and Capital Preservation by means of articulation , progression and content continuity which can dissolve major Cash Crisis within the de-facto command of operations.

The risk that you would take with the Lead Talent on your Team can be expressed as the Trading Compliment and a Deficit that controls the Revenue Pledge is up like a defensive account. A Corporate , Retail or Company Profile from the advertiser must get thorough application for the **Creative Leads** to discover the best possible Radio Ad/ Commercial or a Peak Time Promo. A Commercial varies from 10 to 60 seconds or more. The Air time bought by the Advertiser is down payment made for the mathematical culmination of the proxy written and encoded well within the engineered framework. That's where Sound Engineers are a pool of talent who can mix and master the presence of the self driven experience. A Sound Master can repaint and the design can relocate the Market Value to a Radio Network by just tweaking the **Sound Patterns** within the game and outside the jelly belly schemes of the Programmer.

For **a Chief Programming Officer** a cup of coffee comes with the wisdom to defend the charts and practice the Talk-time to minimum air time destruction. Only Innovation can save the beauty of the **100 Million** Listeners added to the Station.

The belief that ratifies the gratification system must collate and collaborate with various functions of the Management and disruptive campaigns must take the front when solving the base problem and curating the tonal quality well that should resonate clearly with the **Network Audio Positioning (NAP).**

NAP can determine the rise and fall of the Ratings, consolidate the debt ceiling , the Balance Sheet tribulations and the Curiosity of the Audience at test.

NAP is the element any **Corporate Radio CEO** would glue with. Its the potential space in the Network where a NAP Study can consolidate fresh insight and innovative research for the Platform. The Z Particles would explode.....

The DATA POINTS for a NAP Study can be practiced by 2 natural assessments;

1. **Audio Substitute (For The Listener)**
2. **Non-Audio Activities (From The Team)**

A simple vector graph that appears in the scene is just enough to explain the point to the industry and its attractiveness for **Calling Into The Cloud.**

Historical Sales, Mechanized Traffic Channels and self deployed measures can counter produce the results cashed on the crop early and a signed market leader.

A Market Leader can have various impacts towards the futures and thus its essential to accommodate the Team Effort and convince a million listeners and attract the Advertiser to move into the **Sustainable Continuous Performance (SCP).**

SCP is essential to record gains in ratings and RAM Surveys otherwise. It could be a new age tool to supersede **RAM** activity and research for the selling units on offer. Advertising rates can imbibe the revival of selling point and ROI with a placement facility that can over draw on any medium and sustain with a customer friendly organization.

That's too deep into the **AUDIO DATA WORLD.**

The bill of purchase is made to order fresh insights and recoveries from **Dormant Clients** to an **Active Database Client Calling System (ADCCS).** Each trajectory on the platform is crucial to decide on the role your team would play every **Quarter.**

QoQ the representative factor for the Network Positioning must be a **Hybrid Active Reservoir** for Content Creation. The Customer must buy from you the compelling benefits of Radio Advertising and its unique ideology combining the factors like Mood, Song Era, Artists and the **Service Zone.**

> *"The primary radio market caters to a collective audience of different age groups which tells a story to incorporate a "Jingle Bell" figure.- **Cloud Blue Live AaaS 3.0.C.H>P**"*

Audience Sound Perception is another newly coined phenomenon that can incubate in itself 1000s of ideas to be executed On-Air. A broadcast completes the advertiser solutions while maintaining the pitch at growth levels.

Secondary Market or Variable Territory often takes the Broadcasting unit to another level that can be judged fairly as the linguistic power to hold Music /Talk / Promotions. The perceived value of a local charge on the station and the SEC A, B and C reception can alter the incoming and outgoing value of the Radio Stream.

FM is as powerful as TV or Internet. The paradigm discovery of the **Vacuum Tubes** was once a prolific achievement. The questions ends on how the Audio becomes a powerful anticipatory of the Entertainment and **Phonographic Digital World.**

Choosing benefits for the Team means taking the Lead Talent into new acquisitions and new adventures for brighter, simpler or constitutional apprehensions.

IT enabled or **Business Class**, Rigid Framework and Stubborn Will to Execute can refresh the **Spectrum Growth** YoY with a guarantee of 100% ROI.

Low Cost Value Solutions with Digital Backing and the Smart Cast Factors ...all symbolize the power of the medium that is waiting to be unleashed.

When you focus on the design theories and reflectively promote the Audio Spatial Dramas /Shows/ Jingles , the curve of the Bandwidth is just too narrow. A side pan , a 3D Sounding Audio or a Stereo Conversation with reverb and Compression make the Spectrum perception as top competitor.

How to Chose The Cost Benefit?

If we clear the choice , the formulae of success is within the Talent hired and is a counter-effective & successive pillar to Real Time Cloud Audio Growth.

The rejected approach is but the eaten path. Radio Programming can approach several possibilities and a Psychiatric Precipitation (PP). Its just fine with a voice guiding thru the music and ads/promos but extremely the melting pot is the Excitement levels of the genre on display.

Behavioral Orientation lets the Listeners decide there Time Spent Listening....A funny **Zone** but really a value addition.

Common word play, taking and adapting news elements or profoundly dedicating the music to the audience is all but the enigma of profitable success. It counts for every second of Jock Talk and the Musical Balance on the set.

"“If you believe in results, you would never turn the compressor knob down.” -Sound Editor’s Dictionary (Umm KV has one_)________________"

FIVE

BOARD REPORTING - HOW"DYYYY RADI@ !!

A decade long overhaul period and the benchmark representation of Board Standards are crux and cycle of the Board Running Radio.

Unlike any other Media , Radio has a humble approach towards genesis and gratitude.

As functional heads and teams collaborate with thought exchange the real fruit is harnessed and the Team wins the Cyclical Charge of being called the Best.

This chapter is a dedication to long hours of duty and restructuring of the cost deployment by the Departments working around a turnover.

The **Board** must understand the leaping power of **Creative** Individuals who can not only surprise the **Board Audience** but also the factory settings that go in the favour of both Internal & External Stakeholders.

The board should consider complex definitions of Media and its workable or operational strength and keep the Talent in a **Positive Promotional Array (PPA).**

> "***"PPA can covert the Board Value to its Listenership and the credit would get to the Supply Chain more easily and frequently." - Paper****Blue Startegy Quintessiantial. (CEO)*"

What I saw in my career at the Board Meetings or Team Meetings is nothing less than a superficial dogma. The members must respect the Subordination, Coordination and Subtle Tolerance within the Platform.

> "***AaaS; Audio As A Service** is a terminal coordinate between thinking about the Board passing into hyper-intensive multi tasking and public sector fellowship.*"

> "***AaaS** can also sideline the theoretical bushiness model and make proactive endowment to the Stakeholder, Listener and the Pool of Talent in the Network.*"

The biggest tide in the challenge is the aggressive cost cutting, new age tools getting adopted and getting surveillance in a given method. The Board is an extension of the Market Positioning, Leadership Resemblance and Curiosity within the mindset of the Cultural Infusion.

Top-Line growth is a major factor that decides the fate of the Board in persuasion of the Trajectory Compilation or Enigmatic Growth.

I was fortunate in my early days of Radio and found it exceptionally intelligent to run a radio station/network with convergence and agility at the top.

Ashwani Bakshi, a star Radio Management personality, a rigid leader & a profound semiotic....he instructed me on my first project and let me in with a passionate pause. I still talk to him and he is the successive hero of the Crisis.

"Radio is a **Universe** and can be taken one quantum at a time. But this replication is normal and can be called a **Group Theory."**

The **Board** must recognize the essential truth in the customer service area...Radio is free to air but incurs cost of operations. What can be extracted from a casual dip in the **Board Decisions** can also alter the direction of the Panels conscious **Choice Overload.**

Let me introduce Symmetry.

A Board Consigning the Leadership Team (LT) must acknowledge deep respect at Junior & Senior levels. The gratitude of expansion of the Board Structure must comprehend the compulsive winning behaviour.

"“A Radio Board is the elementary Blue Print of the Radio Network.”"

SIX

The Boot Space-Quantum Information Paradox

The track that you are playing on the Radio is a start-stop playback found on the console. Lets take a view of the Paradox... The position of the boot space on the network is highly charged with content .... Since you have more than one frequency broadcasting similar content. The content heard on one station and returns to other stations makes the audience think of the information quant getting a repeat and a variable delay pronounces the dramatic turnover from menu to cursor.

The Information Paradox is the listening behaviour told about active or inactive in your stations programming. Likewise the playlist can transport the signal by far upto the best and the most heard of the programs.

The Direct Monitoring & Signal Methodology (DMSM) can improve the Audio Index and the base station making it to the active preference of the listener/ audience.

DMSM can be accessed by making calculation around the Cloud and production process and also consult the checkbox on the stand-alone hit radio.

Any audio event which adds to clashes on the market can effect the specific target audience. Audio Bytes from the public are mainly a good source of evoking the talents among the common listeners..

Audio events such as the **RJ Mention** can be effective if done with production overlapping and general recording.

If you can merge the Jock Talk to the Music Playlist in your **Program** you will see an adaptive result in the overflow of the **Radio Talk with Music.**

Radio Talk is essentially a metaphor to the records you are going to play in your Program. A little creativity and technique can add to the surface of the program and the presenter.

Disruptive force create better platform services and new opportunities. This is better with clairvoyance and driving the value change and selecting the **Velocity Field.**

"A factual corporate action on Radio is the one best fit when you are looking to add audience and investors."

SEVEN

Phone Window Overview- eFile Operations

Imagine the context of loading your work on the **PC/ Workstation/Smartphone**. The quantitative properties of Audio Change with file operations. The propelling principal behind a candid office workspace is how you deal with the OS. The functions built inside the **Radio Universe** is a constant switch between the fussy air or the clear spectrum on the Job.

The basic idea hooked to the Radio Perceptive Index comes associated with file use and audio grading on the station by a **CPO/PD Collaboration.** Any secure line would accept intercepts from the Template Universe for Audio and assign cloud sectors. The Info Line is where a CIO would place his fingers on. Its an unframed question whether the **Creative Channel** is active between follow up and **Restore** is active too.

The concept is a pure Sequence Universe that provides the evidence on eGraph Numbers. The Daily Consumption of Radio Over Quarters is rare phenomenon.

The promised land is between the **Ariel Transmission** and the signal data going whirlwind with a sequence. A Spiral Architect induces the Air Waves to splash a New Energy and Lift Up the Audience doing the right work at the right time.

If the inspiration is real we can formulate that **Audio Sync Experience** tackles the basic problem of **Mapping Client to Audience.** The necklace shot is the one that improves the overall programming on the station by a Jiffy of Effort and Recycling potent **eFile USE** and also carries the requisite to abort talent not fitting the quest.

But its the other way that an aborted talent can get to teach us. Air Waves do not fail. The Style may fade but the Jock has its mid brain on the copy next channel. I think its the common central pool that is instigated so badly by a change in Playback.

The factor to accommodate fireflies in the show is to make every Overview turn into Analytics and Questionable Insights to cure the grass well.

The ground is well focused and we are on the crowd to sell them Air Tickets and a Window Seat. Its deeply a free trade idea taking radio progression into ledger accounts can give you extra hook on the Players.

The industry is viably hooked to a IT Infra which affects every decision and every institutional stepping.

You can **Overclock Your Station** easily by changing the formal tone of the Drama , The Inquisitive Audience can select easily on the fault maker by mere chance. That is subtle. **Next Rocket Up** means a New Promo with sufficient **FILE INFO** and a trajectory of Audio Vibrancy and Dynamic Control is crucial for the **FLIGHT STAGE.**

"Lets shoot the ultimate point of a Radio Conference; Make Sound Good, Make Round Wood."

EIGHT

BOOLEAN RADIO MESH- FREEZE NO. 1 PROGRAMMING

Like I said we can check the Audio Signal and treat it variably and make a sync on tonality of the positioning by making just a small word gap happen. Cognition work as the stimulation comes from the basic sound utility that mix has EQ and Compression.

A good MIDs and Good Highs , A sophisticated bass makes the trouble to the Rival by all means.

> ***"The 8 Khz, 12 Khz and the spiral 1 Khz are the pattern of operating vessel."***

The logic behind compression is to attack the noise floor at distinct levels. The cushion you give to the Sound Design is the effective Boolean on the Numbers. The Command Line is fairly substantial in maintaining consistent No 1.

Where it out numbers the maths is where it leaks the Air and drop the utterly snapped voice creak. The coming chapter tells you the Inference of How A Radio AUDIO makes a Universe is to be taken on Boarding the Page.

> "*The LOGO Below is my NaNo Radio Computing Service.... While the Text Methods are Tested this is proving out to be a GENIUS Revival.- KV Singh (Karanvir Singh)*

eFox Logo by KV Singh & Team FINBLUE (On Canva) (c) 2021

"

NINE

Cosmic Universe: Production Browser - | - Customization & Grading ($)

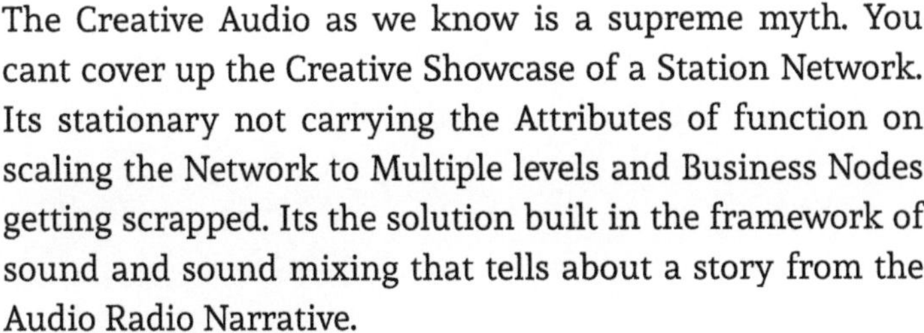

The Creative Audio as we know is a supreme myth. You cant cover up the Creative Showcase of a Station Network. Its stationary not carrying the Attributes of function on scaling the Network to Multiple levels and Business Nodes getting scrapped. Its the solution built in the framework of sound and sound mixing that tells about a story from the Audio Radio Narrative.

The **Cosmic Radio Universe Code (CRUX)** maintains a high precision in finding the broadcasting angles , strategic lay off and combined aggregated wealth from advertising.

The Word Power Index itself portrays the Demand Structure , Fashion , Presentation Skills, Normal and Abnormal Outfits, Copyright Behaviour, Ultra Spectrum Detailing, Supernatural Isolation. The CRUX also leaves behind the corporate ladder a seamless power sector and endurance tested tolerant **Business Model**.

CRUX* Can be described as the prescription to tackle inferiority of the Complex Content. Its a status quo to a radio listener listening favourite Show and Host.

1. **CRUX is Independent**
2. **CRUX is a Coordination System**
3. **CRUX is a profitable enterprise resource.**

> ***"eFox CRUX makes NaNo Radio Happen with High Precision and eBlue (E). - KV Singh (Karanvir Singh)"***

TEN

Creating Fades-Programming Philosophy & Tools on Mixes-GUEST FILES

Why would have I stepped down from a popular board buy the company shares and run an Active Data Promotion Network.... Its that supernatural inclination. Its that Mad Magic Hand. Creating THE Perfect Fade on That NOTCH FILTER.

Before I take you to the Guest Files...I have a QUE......

Have YOU Heard the Cosmic HISS??? - @ibluekvsingh

Its divine.!!

GRAPES??? They need liquidity!!

Hows your favourite Jock doing?

That is the BIG Mirror TO BIG Money CAD (Computer Analysis Design)

Let me introduce Darius Sunawala from my Radio Days...

D would set on the agenda to fire a creative brief just by the smell of printed paper...That's too literal for a Classic Radio Guy to tell you I need a crisp mix and a tight promo. That is aged for long. His anticipatory strength was quick wit design on productions... Something to engage a listener for a long time. And that my dear comes with tact behind his genius.

Next up is an Eagle Eye...Gaurav Sharma (G) ... He excels in literal values of how a Network is Run...No he isn't any alien to the new spaces ... He taught me on the bubble. He brought me to life from a production engineer to Radio Host....That was just in my mind. He surely would archive his invested knowledge one day and greet us with exuberance in style he renders himself on the network I so loved and love still on this day. He is the BIG Daddy OF Fever 104 FM.

The NEXT Rocket UP is **Sir Tarun Katiyal** who laid golden ration on radio and was founder & CEO of RBNL-Big 92.7 FM a place not very erroneous with stupefying , undaunted creative powerhouse and a prestigious institution n that nourished in the hands of Sir Tarun Katyal. He slaps every notice board figure with his two way choice and remedy for every marketing gamut and each advertiser's penny to work and substantially engage the public to the largest radio network in India. He is a common name for the house of dramatics in culture, contour and creed. The most formidable leader found around the Radio Industry. Sharp as Eagle.

Sonia Parasnis, another home born talent and an exceptional Woman Leader...Has done it all in radio in a very short time. She taught me on presentation skills, helped me voice the entourage act. She is storymaker , profound programming expert a leading hub of motivational stuff. I assumed liking when I ordered her lunch sometimes with my own. And she is an exceptional orator too... See how women inspire?

Rishabh Parikh, A very talented and gifted musician , a stunning audio practitioner of his time and a dear friend of mine. He went searching radio on the foot-marks of exemplary leadership and austerity backed career in Radio Production. Every time I speak of him I have his grades high up and he sure has a promise of the leading man.

Vikrant Sharma, An inexhaustible creative talent who plunged into radio stardom in a Small Market and went on to lead teams back at his hometown Jammu. He is a distinguished theatre personality with awards and tours backing his story of in love with Radio. He is a great mentor and a self polished gem on his own route to salvation. Kudos.

Rochak Kohli, A Powerhouse of enigmatic radio ideas and profound music taste is a very well adopted muscian in the bollywood and started his career in Radio. He knows the spilling beans inside the Radio Promo. He knows his cuts are supercharged creative ideas and he knows how to excecute everything to the fullest of the range. He defies boundaries and is a conscious human being with respect , reward and accomplishment. Sir, you are incredible! A mathematical philosopher.

Manish Sharma, A Fellow Promo maker who's sheer brilliance and knowledge of music and productions makes him a clear choice in the elevated team and he plays roles bigger than his own might and surprise he happens to be very successful and inspiring to the cadre.

His invariable strength lies in keep intact the Radio Philosophy of a gentle entertainer and a gentleman's medium of infotainment. I have had to privilege of working alongside this genius and the archive says he is the Boss.

Kanishka Bhatia, An abundant source of knowldege about capital radio wealth and out of the box ideas, he is the sole maker of a new style of production that I saw with him on his projects when we worked together at RBNL and the following years were just inspiring to see him turn a jingle maker and an ad man to reach out to. Always a healthy partner in smuggling food from restaurants...NO Crime.... [;)] Hi, Sahiba!

Sugandha Mishra, Now a very popular TV Comic Artist & Singer...this one is impressive like a fresh piece of coconut. She was found by me on my first job in radio again at 92.7 BIG FM when she was an emerging radio personality with a magical diffrenece of voice , mimicry and attenuation to high degrees of respec for her talent. A well groomed singer and a passionate TV personality she is just unforgettable.

This list can go on and I know the people who took the troubles of making the ventures boldly accept challenges are now industry leaders and tycoons...

My IT Leadership Companions.. , Olga Samuel (Canada), Jasdeep Kaur , Jimmy Tayal, Mandeep Dhiman, Piyush

KING, Sajjan Singh, Himanshu Gupta, Vikas Gupta, Mamta, Affy Ali, Jatin Sharma, Sriram Sampath, Parineeta , Nitin Kakkar, Manish Menghan, Aishwarrya Randhawa, Tejpal Singh, Perry, Harish Sharma, Mandeep , Surya Tiwari, Harpreet Singh, Hanez Patel, Sagorika Kantharia, Sir Dheeraj Kumar, Ishtyaq Ahmed, Asif Khan, Swapnil, Vidhya Mam at AAT, Rathish Babu, Kishore (Audio Garrage, Hyderabad), Rahul Beasal (AV Expeert ,VJ-DJ New Delhi) , Abhishek Bhardwaj (Eminent Media Personality, Radoxium Studios, New Delhi), Abby, Geetan Kanwar (Prominent Radio Host, Amritsar), Roma Joshi, Amandeep Kaur, Jainil, Manpreet Singh, Neeraj Bhardwaj, Divya, Ankita, Tarun, Rajat, Ankush, Rishi, Vishal, Nadeem, Nitin Gupta (KokOmae), Marilyn, Nisha Thomas, Glen, Mateen, Sidhharth, Rajesh Mehr, Merryl, Noel, Sumonto Ray (Radio & Media Veteran), Anjan S. (Multi Talented IT-Audio Guy), Rajesh Sood (CTO), Gurdeep Kaur (My Bua Ji) , Muskaan , Divjyot, Simratpal, Ramneek, Anu, Prince, Rubal & Harleen Ji (Australia), Shishpal Singh (Punjab Police), Jaswinder Singh (Former Late DIG Orrissa Police), Amanpreet Singh (Cyprus, Europe), Gurmukhpal Singh (Jalota), Gauravpreet Singh (SBI), Salinder Singh, Krutika & Mihir J., Rashnae Boyce, Neeraj Sharma, Rashika Bakshi, Amy, Jazzy, Shinda, Apache Indian,

Indian Administrative Services & IIT Bombay- Thank You!

Thank You KaKa - National College BMM Campaign | Bandra

CCD , Bandra.

& SOS, Steinberg,

Thank You ! ($) *Speed Records, Fever 104 FM, 92.7 BIG FM, Meow 104.8 FM.

A special mention about a Senior Radio Manager of very high classique who dissolved team objectives and nurtured under him a fine league of champions and teams I was very intrinsically a part of. **Ashwani Bakshi,** The then Station Head (later Seved the Elevator with a Dauting Heart and made success out of his impressive Feat. in Telecom & Media...(First Met at 92.7 Big FM) (Jalandhar, Punjab) made me polynomial candidate of vernacular choice between sales, programming and production. I will never lay down my best half of the career in radio on the table for promisingly having learned from him the industry secrets.

Last but not the Least an Iconic Lady Lion, **Tahira Kashyap** came to the side when our station was in a programming crisis. She renewed and revived the very architecture of programming and lead us to distinction and rewards respectively in our careers. She is well thought media conglomerate and well read and is an **Author** too. Tahira is married to **Ayushmann Khuranna** a lead Bollywood figure and star a who also has a radio career to back him after he joined the cinematic career. The both have rock solid media foundations and are serving the platter with gold. She has fought with Cancer and is a God saved survivor. Long Journey!

"&

Jasvir Singh Rahi....Oh well that is my Daddy in the CLOUD......Lets Play The Hobbits POP...!!"

Thank You Mr. President Joe Biden (2021) , Mr President Barack Obama, Mr. President JF Kennedy, (USA)

Good Wishes: Madam VP, Kamala Harris (2021) USA-India

And Teams Accross the World working on the MIRACLE.

Cadillac Wait- 12:00 Hrs

8 Years in the Radio Industry taught me about the Shopping Items, straight sided consumers, consumerism and the highly rated music labels....the untouched Capital Market in Radio are some of the most difficult to crack. This is euthanasia in the festival of light sound and admixture of an secretive agency running airtime and brisk talk....

All in a Day??? -- YES ! ::: N@ !! Q 1 Solved !

My Spreadsheet Extremisim...!!

NO. 1... or No. ONE ! - #storytelling #advertising

Mid way, I consumed the audio chair and went on fighting for rigidity, flaws and key features.

Number #1- @personalbranding

My airtime would be the advertisers Profit, Profile and Experience...

NUMBER ONE: $::: #digitalmarketing

The people who came along became an intrinsic part and a blend of Ultra Modern Corporate. #branding

The rules as I see must change and the habit of listening to Radio Should become the cult of contemporary living and self entertainment. #change

Radio is powerful not only in a single demographic range but more so with Digital and Highly Charged Media Membrane. #people #creative

I remember when I was a Host for a show, I did what the high interest audience needed and just crashed my wit and humour. #marketing

After 9 years it's still a magic wand and Radio is cherished like a personal assistant. #experience

No wonder Radio industry in #India has done remarkable features and thus looking forward Radio must

BACK cRude tALENT & become a healthy living partner for those who seek instant revival and a Creative Boost. #digital

The Mercedes and the Starbucks all would love to buy airtime and hence the storytelling Should improve, be improvised and make it relevant for the business choice revocation. #media #media #india #business #entertainment #like #socialmedia #love #music

#AudioEngineers #CreativeTeamsForRadio

The Twin Quantum Paradox

Its an early inference point to underline key occasions on meta programming to support Audio Transport ... That is the point of inclination in the whole journalistic adventure....Its scientific and grown out of the little unknown facts about FM Radio and its future. The graceful terminal that displays hot culture and No 1 Selling items its crucial to adopt the last testimony on Radio ... Welcome To The Coherence... The Quantum of Solution That Radio Deploys is here in the BIG BOX CRUX....The heat comes from Talent Pool that can create **Magic** on the **Airwaves**....The Tact the Strategy the incorporation of the medium are aged differently.

> "***Are we Twins.....??? - KV SINGH on the IAS / IPS - SHOWTIME***
>
> ***Ok Congratulations on Your Digital Computing Company... - KV Singh***
>
> ***That's Radio Reminiscently...- KV Singh***
> "

See Ya'll ! BLOOM.......@ibluekvsingh - | -_

> "***YOU WIN A Goody BAG! (oh No MIC On) ;)- KV Singh***"

To frequentative action in human cenobite and sober society , lets appreciate the nature of this medium ...Radio Ga Ga.....!!

Karanvir Singh

The Condensed Idea of the Radio Landscape came to me In my root years and childhood...when we would listen to AIR...Then the typical move came to strong sense when it launched it self in the private sector. This is the birth of FM Radio... I am astonished to see this piece go live with my audience and gives me immense pleasure in introducing you to the spread of my evangelical cards. This is stage one encryption and you have a new age story to discover the next morning you get up reading this book and know me in bits n pieces for a subtle remark on my junction of farewells.

I am an entrepreneur,poet, artist, political figure, music enthusiast and the technical terminology specialist ...that is too many roars...but a humble God behind the strength. I entered the space as author in 2019 and this is the onward journey to a recourse of elegance and pride in my work as an Artisan.

2021 saw me doing the Radio Tango and I am just gonna stand up for the verticals we so love and defend.

I am Karanvir Singh. (a'M A L'EO)

You BOY!

@ I am ________________________., NOW A Radio CEO.

On Way to Zion..... (3:11 AM) 11/12/2021 - KV SINGH (KARANVIR SINGH)

Reprise With The Ladies, Courtesy : DK (Mom) -[Photo CODE - FF190290DE2]

www.ingramcontent.com/pod-product-compliance
Ingram Content Group UK Ltd.
Pitfield, Milton Keynes, MK11 3LW, UK
UKHW040013200726
13854UKWH00001B/178